Forgiveness

The Healing Power Of Forgiveness

*Discover How To Use The Power Of
Forgiveness To Truly Live A Much
Happier, Productive And Fulfilling Life*

By Ace McCloud

Copyright © 2014

Disclaimer

The information provided in this book is designed to provide helpful information on the subjects discussed. This book is not meant to be used, nor should it be used, to diagnose or treat any medical condition. For diagnosis or treatment of any medical problem, consult your own physician. The publisher and author are not responsible for any specific health or allergy needs that may require medical supervision and are not liable for any damages or negative consequences from any treatment, action, application or preparation, to any person reading or following the information in this book. Any references included are provided for informational purposes only. Readers should be aware that any websites or links listed in this book may change.

Table of Contents

DEDICATED TO THOSE WHO ARE PLAYING THE GAME OF LIFE TO

KEEP ON PUSHING AND NEVER GIVE UP!

Ace McCloud

Be sure to check out my website for all my Books and Audio books.

www.AcesEbooks.com

Introduction

I want to thank you and congratulate you for buying the book, "Forgiveness: The Healing Power of Forgiveness– Discover How to Use the Power of Forgiveness To Truly Live a Much Happier, Productive and Fulfilling Life."

This book contains proven steps and strategies on how to forgive others and yourself. This will allow you to stop dealing with the pain of old wounds and heal them once and for all. Once this is done, you can become much more productive and be happy and unencumbered by resentment and anger.

The act of forgiveness is not an easy thing to do. You have been wronged. Your emotions are in turmoil. Whatever the offender did, it took you from a calm, peaceful life and threw you into an unpleasant, dramatic situation that upset your everyday life. How do you move on and get past this?

Forgiveness is a process that frees the mind of negative emotions in order to restore peace and harmony in life. It does not mean everything goes back comfortably to the way it was. It just means that you accept what happened, you stop rehashing the event over and over and you can regain the strength to carry on without resentment and anger. Forgiveness also allows for healing and helps you to move on to bigger and better things in life.

Gerald G. Jampolsky, MD, author, physician, psychiatrist and founder of the International Center for Attitudinal Healing said, "Forgiveness is the key to peace and happiness, and is the greatest healer of all." Without forgiveness, the world would be a horrible place full of anger and fear. Having the ability to forgive is a great attribute. Holding a grudge over someone only holds onto the past and does not allow one to progress pleasantly towards the future. Grudges prevent healing and allow hate to fester.

I knew a woman that thought she married the most wonderful man in the world. Unfortunately, he cheated on her and she found out about the affair. She got a divorce and that should have been the end of it, but she was so consumed by the betrayal, she could not move forward. She tried to date other men, but she continued to dwell on the experience and believed all men were the same. She trusted no one and even went as far as planning revenge on her ex-husband. She could have been doing something much better with her energy and she will never know all the great relationships she may have missed out on by being so consumed by anger and hatred. Ultimately, she drifted away from the church, lost most of her friends and now lives alone just going out of the house to go to work and back.

Forgiveness frees the soul and the mind. In some cases it is said to reduce blood pressure and heart rate. Forgiving someone may help you to sleep at night instead of tossing and turning as you think about the past. Forgiveness can reduce anger, depression and anxiety, however, it is not something that can be turned on and off at will - like a light switch. You have to work at it.

Sometimes it takes a few weeks to forgive someone for what they have done. Other times it takes longer. It all depends on the person and the circumstances. It is much easier to forgive someone for eating what you put aside for your lunch at the office than to forgive someone who drove drunk and killed a family member. You can't force yourself to forgive too soon. If you aren't ready, you will not get the results that are needed to set you free and promote healing. Working some of the exercises in this book and understanding methods of forgiving will prepare your heart to finally forgive.

Some things that prevent forgiveness include anger, being afraid of the circumstance happening again and, therefore, being unwilling to forgive and forget and having an ego that won't allow forgiveness. The offended person might be comfortable being considered a victim and enjoy the attention. They may not want to admit that they were hurt for fear that they will be embarrassed or they may be in denial saying that they do forgive someone when they didn't actually go through the process and the resentment still burns within them. They may think the offender does not deserve forgiveness because of the act or because they are not sincere about being sorry. All of these things tend to prevent forgiveness from happening and it might be a long time before a person can move past them.

Forgiving someone does not mean the circumstance or incident was right or justified. You can't take back what happened. True forgiveness does not erase the issue. Instead, the issue is accepted. All the emotional upheaval created by this issue is gone and no longer rehashed over and over. Trust, however, may have to be earned again and may never be totally regained.

Jack Kornfield is a teacher and author that trained as a Buddhist monk in Thailand. He teaches all kinds of techniques for healthy, positive living and he has a humorous and helpful YouTube video called the 12 principles of Forgiveness by Greater Good Science Center. In this video, he teaches what forgiveness is and gives very good examples.

To forgive is to heal broken fences and be able to look to the future instead of dwelling in the past. Mahatma Gandhi said, "The weak can never forgive. Forgiveness is the attitude of the strong." Forgiveness might be the hardest thing you have ever done, but once you have done it, your life will be lighter, happier, and much better!

Chapter 1 – Express Emotion and Control it

When you feel betrayed, a gambit of emotions engulfs you. Anger is usually directed against the offender and against the situation. Hate might be an initial emotion directed at the offender. Disappointment is another emotion that arises. The thought of "how could anyone do that to me?" might pop into your head. Distrust might be an issue that plays against the offender. Once the anger wears off, sadness rolls in and can melt your body and soul into a puddle of tears. Crying, screaming and shouting are all good ways to get all that emotion out into the open. It cleanses and allows you to think more objectively about the situation.

Whenever you feel frustrated and angry, expressing that anger by crying or screaming into a pillow can actually help. It releases pent up steam and might even lower your blood pressure. Drive out into the country and let loose with a long yell.

Expelling emotion is very helpful, but also be cautious with it or you might offend someone else and you will be the one that needs to be forgiven. The following techniques and suggestions should help you on the road to forgiveness by expressing emotions and giving you the ability to control them.

Write a Letter
Write a long letter to the offender. Tell them how you feel about the injustice they committed. Go into detail and explain why it was so wrong for them to do what they did. Once you are done writing, read the letter back and decide if you want to send it to the offender or not. Should you decide to not send the letter, you can burn it, rip it into shreds or bury it. You might find this action very healing.

Talk to the Offender
Telling the offender how you feel might benefit you by releasing emotion and, the good thing is, they don't even have to be present to do it. You can express your emotion to an empty chair or ask a trusted friend to stand in for the offender. Scream, yell and discuss whatever makes you feel better. If you should decide to directly talk to the person that hurt you and you want to retain a relationship with them, make sure to be careful. You don't want to get so intense you permanently offend them. Try to word things more diplomatically. You may have to practice prior to speaking directly to them. Practice using more controlled words and speaking into a mirror. Watch your body language and decide what you will actually say and do before you confront anyone personally. Try not to come off as being an offender yourself, which may take a few days for you to cool down to do so.

A good method that will help you decide what to say is to write the letter and tone it down for a discussion. The word "you" can be very confrontational so be careful how you use it. Instead of accusing the other person of being a selfish idiot, reason with them. Your discussion might look a little like this:

"I did not appreciate it when I asked you to take me to the grocery store and you didn't have time and wanted me to pay gas money. Maybe you didn't realize my car was in the shop for several days and I had no way to get around. My kids were hungry and I had no food to feed them. I feel your insensitivity to my problem might cause me to ignore your plea to help to you when you need it."

This discussion is still telling the offender how you feel, but you are doing it in a calmer fashion. This will get you much further than attacking them and calling them names.

The anger and other strong emotions you have at first when an incident happens, do serve a purpose. They are there to encourage you to do something instead of letting strong negative feelings fester and burn in your soul.

Author and theologian, Lewis B. Smedes said, "Healthy anger drives us to do something; to change what makes us angry; anger can energize us to make things better. Hate wants to make things worse."

Emotion Calming Exercise

When hostile emotion takes over, use this exercise to calm the feelings that are emerging so that you don't lash out and do something you may regret.

1. Breathe – When you experience strong emotion, breathing becomes labored, quick or may stop all together. When you realize you are breathing erratically, take control. Close your eyes and concentrate only on your breath. Hopefully you aren't driving or doing something that would distract focus. If so, stop and make sure everything is safe first.

2. Once breathing is under control, start counting your breaths. Breathe deeply and purposefully and count to ten. By this time your breathing should be totally under control.

3. If your heart is beating swiftly and you feel tense, you need to relax. Start at the neck and force your muscles to let go and relax little by little all the way down to your feet. This will do much to lower your heart rate and help you relax enough to deal sensibly with the issue.

The explosion of emotion can make a sensible person do crazy, insane things. It is important to calm yourself before you do or say anything. On the other hand, expressing emotion helps to externalize issues instead of internalizing them. It is healthy to get angry as long as it is kept in check. Turn those raw emotions into forgiveness.

Chapter 2 – Feel Love and Gratitude

Love and gratitude go a long way in giving a person the ability to forgive. You can't solve anything for yourself or others through hate and vengeance. Dr. Martin Luther King, Jr. said, "We must develop and maintain the capacity to forgive. He who is devoid of the power to forgive is devoid of the power to love. There is some good in the worst of us and some evil in the best of us. When we discover this, we are less prone to hate our enemies."

This does not mean you have to love the person that caused you pain, although you may. You just have to resist the temptation to hate them. The power of love is absolutely amazing. Many of the problems in our world today could be solved if people would exhibit a little more love.

Gratitude is the great ice breaker in the scheme of life. Once you start thinking of all the things you have to be grateful for, it is difficult to focus on retribution and hate.

Happiness is internal, not external. It comes from within and love and gratitude help to bring out happiness instead of loathing and hate. Try some of the following exercises to encourage feelings of love and gratitude in your daily life.

Gratitude Inventory

1. Take a piece of paper and number 1 through 10 down the left margin. Write down the top 20 things you are most grateful for now at this moment. It might be your kids, your spouse, a loving mom and dad, your job, your friends, your home, or thousands of other things. Dig deep to find all those things that you enjoy in life from people and pets to material objects and abilities that you possess.

2. Take another piece of paper and number it from 1 to 20 down the left margin. Write in all the things you were grateful for before the incident for which you must forgive happened. You can use some of the same things on the first list.

3. Now that you have finished both lists, you should feel better and be more centered on happiness and gratitude than you were on anger and retribution. It is amazing how distracting oneself from the issue takes away all that negativity and replaces it with a peaceful calmness.

4. Look at your lists. What is different? If your spouse cheated on you, you might not put him or her on the second list since you are more than likely not too grateful for them at the moment. In all probability, your two lists are not too different. One little bobble in life should not make such a huge difference. It is miniscule in the large scheme of things, especially if your insensitive mother-in-law and her busy-body attitude is the problem.

Some issues like a cheating spouse are more difficult to get over, but you still have all those other things on your lists to be grateful for and to back you up and make you happy.

Make a Love List

Another exercise that will help open your eyes and mind to all the love and happiness in the world is to make a love list.

1. Write down all the people you love. Include relatives, friends and pets. Now write down all the things you love. It might be your vegetable or flower garden, the kids you coach in baseball or your new vehicle.

2. Make a list of all the people, places and things you want get to know and love including the person you want to forgive. You might want to have a friendly relationship with your new neighbor, so write that down. You might want to go to Tahiti and love it there, so write it down.

3. Close your eyes and visualize each of those people you love and then think about all the things that you love one at a time. When this is done, try to visualize all the things you want to love. Now, visualize the offender and try to keep your anger at bay. After thinking about all the lovely things in your life, it should be easier to achieve this. Think about all the things you loved about that person. This should help you to either let the person go and be done with everything or to recreate a relationship with them. You may start to realize over time that your anger might be a trivial thing in the entire scheme of things. That is for you to decide rationally. This might help you to decide you need to forgive the person because it isn't worth all the hate and anger anymore. You loved them once, so maybe you can give them the benefit of the doubt and stop hating them so much.

You cannot force yourself to love someone when you have bad feelings for them. However, those bad feelings might be conquered by love.

Perhaps you told your best friend that you were going to apply for a job and that friend goes out and applies for the same job and gets it. Maybe your friend's actions were unforgivable, but do you know all the circumstances? Your love for your friend warrants asking for an explanation instead of planning retribution and hate.

It is difficult to have fond feelings for someone that has betrayed you, but your love list may rekindle some of those feelings you had, or at least make things more manageable. When you feel pain, you should not do anything to create more pain. Try to do an act of love instead.

Perhaps you could purchase a congratulations card for your friend since she did get the job, or you could make cookies and take them over to her house. Acts of love make way for forgiveness whereas getting even only makes your heart grow darker. Acts of love and gratitude help you to stop focusing on the act that created the problem and helps you to move on with life.

Chapter 3 – Switch Perspective

Henry Wadsworth Longfellow wrote, "If we could read the secret history of our enemies, we should find in each man's life sorrow and suffering enough to disarm all hostility." What he was saying is that there are two sides, or perspectives, to every story. You know why you feel you have been wronged, but do you know why the offender did what he or she did? You might be surprised at the reason and your heart may be softened by it.

Empathy, or feeling for another person, tends to make it easier to forgive them. Instead of considering the offender the enemy, take the time to look at what precipitated the incident. If you don't know, ask someone who does or go to the offender and ask. You don't know what another person is thinking unless you are a psychic, and in many cases you will find there were no evil intentions. The offender truly was not out to screw you.

Let's look at our former best friend that knew you were trying to get a job and they snatched it away from you. You probably have a perfect right to be upset with them, but stop and think. Did you ever tell them not to interview or did you mention that this job meant a great deal to you? You may have said something as simple as you couldn't go out because you were interviewing for the accountant position at XYZ Company and had to prepare. You may have never said you really wanted the job because the company was close to home, had day care for worker's kids or that it was really hard to put food on the table with the job you currently had. Your friend should have known, but the fact is, some people just don't think unless something is black and white. You didn't tell her not to say anything about the job and you may not have even told her where the job was and it is a coincidence that she applied for the same job.

You may not know the circumstances that precipitated the act. This friend didn't have kids to feed and she lives with her mother. You don't understand why she needed this job so bad that she would jeopardize your friendship. Maybe her mother is going into nursing care and your friend will soon be homeless unless she finds a job to make enough money for rent. Granted, she should have said something, but probably didn't because you did not convey how important it was to you.

Switching perspectives allows you to see both sides of the story. This may help you decide if forgiveness is warranted.

Perspective Exercise

Think about the situation and either write the particulars down or tell an impartial friend, who actually knows both sides of the story, how everything happened. What exactly did you say and do? Now turn around and write or tell the story from the offender's point of view. Pretend you are the offending friend.

Here is an example:

> "I told Mary that I was very happy to have an interview for the accounting position at XYZ Company. She wanted to go out that night, but I had to stay in to prepare and get well rested. She was disappointed, but said she understood. She said she did not know I was looking for another job and I told her I did not make enough money at my current job and was looking."

Now change the perspective. You are now Mary and you do not know all the particulars from the event:

> "My friend told me about an accounting opening at XYZ Company. I'm going to apply because I have an accounting degree and she doesn't. I have experience in accounting and she's been spending that last 5 years being a housewife. She doesn't have a chance in getting the job if I apply. If she doesn't like it, it is just too bad."

Hopefully your impartial friend knows all the particulars and will help you through this exercise by reminding you of Mary's perspective. After hearing the perspective you might write this in Mary's perspective:

> "My friend told me she was interviewing for an accounting job at XYZ company. That is a great place to work because they pay well and have great benefits. Mom is going into nursing care next week and the house will be up for sale the first of next month. I have to do something quick so I have somewhere to live. I think I will send in an application too. They might need more than one accountant and my friend said she was just looking."

Now you can see why it wasn't a big deal for Mary to try and get the job. You are still a little upset, but it is much easier to forgive her because you see her perspective.

Another way to switch perspectives on the situation is to turn evil into good. Maybe something good actually came out of not getting that position with XYZ Company.

Maybe you have done something in your life for which you were forgiven. Think of how it felt to wrong someone. Hopefully you didn't mean to do it, and if you did, you felt regret. Think of how it felt to be forgiven. Being forgiven for something that caused another person to have pain is very humbling. It is also a big relief. It is great to know that the offender still cares about you. You also know you must strive to regain the trust of that person. Switching perspective makes you develop empathy for the offender. It allows you to put the incident into perspective and might heal a shaky relationship in the process.

Chapter 4 – Let Go

Alexandra Asserly was raised in both Beirut Lebanon and London England. Just some of the things she is known for is her psychotherapy work that concentrated on conflict resolution and helping people through painful memories by drawing from her experience during the Lebanese Civil War. One of her most notable quotes is, "Forgiveness allows us to let go of pain in the memory and if we let go of the pain in the memory, we can have the memory but it does not control us. When memory controls us, we are then the puppets of the past." I don't know about you, but I do not want to be a puppet and certainly not one of the past.

The Aramaic word for forgive is equal to the English word "untie". If you untie yourself from the bindings of resentment and let go or forgive, you release yourself from the control the offender has over you. No one likes to think they are controlled by anyone or anything, but holding on tight to anger and resentment only hurts yourself and gives permission for the offender to have control and use you like a puppet.

Some people, including me, find it very difficult to let go of a grudge. Interestingly enough, it is much harder to keep carrying the grudge and not let go than it is to forgive someone. One of the main reasons I wanted to do this book is because I wanted to move forward in life at peak performance and found that painful memories and bad relationships were holding me back. When you are busting your butt to get better every day, improve your life, and become a better human being it is very easy to get angry at other people who try to get through life by lying, cheating, being manipulative, sneaky, etc. The truth is, the majority of people on this planet are operating at nowhere near their full potential, so, unfortunately, the ability to forgive and move on is an absolutely critical skill.

Many do not want to let go of malice they feel for someone who wronged them because they are afraid the offender will repeat the action and hurt them again. Letting go does not mean you condone the action. You can still put in place some protective actions for the future so the situation will not happen again.

Perhaps a co-worker takes credit for all the work you did on a project in order to better his position in the company. He fails to mention all the legwork and research you did and how you produced all those great graphs. Your coworker gets a promotion within the department and you get more work. You can internalize everything and hold a grudge. You might even refuse to help them with another project. This would obviously start friction and letting go in order to forgive them would be impossible, especially if you have to work with this person every day. Take a protective action and request a transfer to another department or location in the company if you can. Not having to be subject to the same behavior makes it much easier to let go and forgive when you know they can't do the same thing to you again.

You might have to make a conscious effort to let go and when you do, it isn't ⸢
to keep bringing the details of the issue up and rubbing it in the offender's f⸢
Of course, it may not seem fair to you to let go and forgive the offender eit⸢
Life isn't always fair. If it makes you feel better, you can believe the offender⸢
get what he is due on judgment day. Job is a character in the Bible. He probably
did not think God was being fair to him when he smote him and took his family,
home and belongings from him. Yet Job let go of his frustration and anger and
remained faithful to God. He forgave Him. In return, God gave Job more than
he had before. Job 11: 13-16 says, "Put your heart right, reach out to God.... then
face the world again, firm and courageous. Then all your troubles will fade from
your memory like floods that are past and remembered no more." Your offender
may not be God. He or she is but a mere human being, but once you let go and
forgive you will find healing and pretty soon you will no longer remember the
event.

Up In Smoke Exercise

Remember that letter you wrote to the person that angered you? Take that letter
that detailed all the pain and resentment you feel and burn it. As the smoke rises,
let all the negative feelings in your heart rise with the smoke and let them
dissipate in the air. This will symbolically signal that you have let go.

Stop reliving the situation and let it go. When you start remembering what
happened, try a visualization exercise.

Letting Go Visualization

1. Lie down and close your eyes. Visualize the person that hurt you and the
   situation.

2. Notice your heart rate rising and your muscles tense.

3. Let go of the vision and concentrate on relaxing your muscles. Do some
   deep breathing by breathing in through the mouth making your stomach
   inflate and breath out through the nose and watch your stomach go flat as
   you exhale. Focus totally on breathing and do at least five to six breathes.

4. Keep your eyes closed and visualize someone you love while allowing your
   mind to fill with pleasurable experiences connected to this person. Notice
   that your heart rate has slowed and your muscles are relaxing. Continue to
   do deep breathing.

5. Switch back to visualizing the offender, but try to keep residual good
   feelings from visualizing a loved one. The offender should not bring about
   such strong reactions because you have distracted yourself.

Practice this exercise and pretty soon you will find the resentment surrounding the offender is severely mineralized. You can let go now and start to heal.

Make a Contract with Yourself

A contract is a binding document that most people respect. Making a contract with yourself subconsciously helps you to let go and start healing again. Draw up a contract. A sample could read like this:

I, (name), hereby grant forgiveness to (name of offender). I forgive them for: (fill in the situation).

Sign and date the contract, fold it up and put it somewhere where it will not be disturbed, or burn it if it makes you feel better.

Throwing Stones

Another exercise to let go involves collecting some flat stones. Clean them up and use acrylic paint to paint on the offender's name and any other words you might associate with the offender. You might write job stealer, selfish, self-absorbed and other such words on them. After the stones dry, wrap them in a square of fabric and tie it up into a pouch with twine or string. Take the pouch in your hand and concentrate on the offender and the situation. Throw that pouch over a cliff or into a river or lake or some other place that it will never be found again. While physically throwing the pouch, mentally throw away and let go of the pain.

Access a YouTube video from a Forgiveness Course Online by Dr. Stephen Marmer, Ph.D, from Prager University by clicking on Forgiveness. This video imparts very good information on three types of forgiveness including severe incidents like child abuse and other violence. It discusses letting go and the damage that can be done by keeping it all inside.

When you do let go, you are no longer a victim. You become an equal with the offender and forgiveness and healing is not far away.

Chapter 5 – Positive Thinking

Albert Einstein said, "You can't solve a problem by staying in the same energy in which it was created." He was right. If a situation was created in negativity, it will never be solved by continuing with negative thoughts. It takes positive energy to resolve.

For many people, it is human nature to think the worst and to dwell on things that bother them. It usually takes a mental shove to get them thinking in a positive manner after a bad thing happens. When negative thoughts cloud the mind, it is good to stop, switch gears and take the role of a bystander instead of a participant by examining thoughts and sifting out the negative ones and replacing them with positive thoughts and feelings.

Sometimes feeling positive is harder than other times. Just remember that positive people are often more happy and healthy than those walking around with a dark rain cloud over their heads. Positive people tend to be less angry, repel stress more easily, be more calm, have the ability to see opportunities more clearly, be less anxious and have a better overall outlook on life. Several studies have proved that those with positive attitudes have less chance of cardio vascular disease and do not get sick as often as negative thinkers do. They are also much happier throughout any given day!

I'm sure you have known some negative thinkers. Did you want to be around them much? Probably not. Those people that are positive draw people like a magnet (pun intended). If you stay positive, you will draw positive people and situations to you and you will forget all about the pain the offender caused. It will become easy to forgive and you will be able to heal.

Negativity blocks energy. It drains energy from every pore in your body. Negativity makes it hard to remember and enjoy the past and think of the future. Just one little negative thought can breed and snowball into a big, fat, negative event in your life. Negativity makes forgiveness and healing impossible.

Revenge is negative, so stop thinking of ways to get back at the person who wronged you. You will never have the ability to forgive as long as you entertain thoughts of retribution. Your coworker, Joe, is the one that took credit for all the work you did on a presentation at work and he was the one that got the promotion. Trying to think up ways to get back at him is time wasted. It happened and you can't do anything about it. Deal with it by using some positive thinking. Joe is really good at speaking and he did an excellent job at the presentation. Your company was awarded the account over other agencies. That is a good thing. Focus on the positive aspects of the incident. Besides, if Joe took credit for everything intentionally, staying positive about the whole thing is the best revenge you can dish out. He won't be able to stand it.

Positive Goals

Set yourself a positive goal and set a period of time in which to attain the goal. You might set a goal of being able to talk pleasantly to Joe in a week. You would prepare by smiling at him whenever you see him and keeping any animosity at bay. Pretty soon you'll be in the lunch room discussing the local football game.

Cutting the Negativity Cord

Make a list of all the people for which you harbor a grudge. It might be just one person or it may be many. Close your eyes and visualize each of them standing around you and connected to you with a black cord. Imagine that you have a pair of golden scissors and you cut the cord. When you do, the cord dissipates in a cloud of dust and you float away from these people freely. You are ridding yourself of that negative cord and it no longer encumbers you from forgiveness, healing and the life you wish to lead. This should help you to let go and give you the ability to forgive.

Journal

Keep a journal and write down all the facts, in the most neutral manner possible, right after an incident happens. Timing is important in this task, so keep a blank notebook handy for this purpose and write everything down immediately. Once you are finished, put that journal away somewhere and try not to think of the incident and stay positive. Take the journal back out after a month or so and read over the incident keeping a positive attitude. Write down what has happened in a positive vein since the incident originally happened and things that might be related to the incident. Your significant other may have cheated on you and you broke up. Since that happened, you may find some positive factors have cropped up. You might have a better relationship with a relative because he or she hated your X. Maybe you have a better relationship because you went to them for consolation. Since you had to move out of your ex's apartment, you may have found a better place to live and just maybe you have found someone else and are in a much better relationship. You might have missed all these positive things if you would have stewed in pain and not gone on with your life

Meditation

It might sound silly, but little positive affirmations can do wonders for a positive attitude. Write down some positive quotes on little cards and place them around the house. When you see one, pick it up and meditate on the quote for a few minutes. You can also participate in a meditation session by focusing on positive feelings. Repeat a mantra of "Love, forgiveness, healing, peace," while breathing deeply.

Smile Therapy

Smiling can make even the most negative thoughts dissipate from your head. Read a humorous story or watch a sit-com on TV. Immediately after, think of the person you wish to forgive and keep smiling. It might be a forced smile, but it is a smile nonetheless. If you see the offender, smile at them. Keep your thoughts positive to heal wounds and allow you to forgive.

Laughter and Humor Therapy

This type of therapy can be very beneficial. For full details on how to do this, be sure to check out my book: Laughter and Humor Therapy.

Change the Inner Dialog

Most people have a running conversation going on in their heads and when you are hurting, the dialog may be negative in nature. Try and keep this conversation positive even when you think about the person that hurt you. Avoiding all negative dialogue goes a long way in being able to forgive that person. A great way to do this is by using positive affirmations. A positive affirmation is a phrase that you repeat over and over in your head to program in positivity and to try and block out negativity. For example: "I am super strong, happy, healthy, and pain free." Or "I forgive quickly, easily and move on to better things."

Hypnosis

Hypnosis has been found to be very effective with forgiveness. My absolute favorite place to get hypnosis audio sessions from is Hypnosis Downloads. They have some great downloadable audios that deal specifically with forgiveness, such as the learn how to forgive download.

Practice Positivity

Instead of spewing negative comments about the person who wronged you, regale others with good comments extolling their virtues. Your mother-in-law might be the most disagreeable pain in the world, but instead of dwelling on her faults, extol her good attributes. She is a good cook, she keeps the house so clean you can eat off the floor, she does good work in her church and would just about do anything for her kids and grandchildren.

Staying positive can set the stage for forgiveness. It is not impossible and when you do it, you become a better, more positive and forgiving person because of it.

Chapter 6 – Understand and Learn About Forgiveness

How can you expect to forgive someone until you have all the facts? It is your duty to learn and understand why the person who committed the transgression did so in order to forgive, especially if it is not within the realm of their normal behavior. There may be extenuating circumstances that precipitated the situation. The offender may not be aware of their betrayal and again, it may have been intentional. Until you learn and understand all the facts of the situation, it is difficult to decide what type of forgiveness to give him or her. Learning and understanding is an integral part of the process.

We need explanations. It is human nature to seek understanding and even if the explanation isn't what we desire to hear, we still need it to allow us to move forward. Was the betrayal retribution for something we did? Was it just a mean spirited fling or was it just for fun. You need the information to start the process of forgiveness, but you also need it to learn from the situation so that it won't happen again.

Here is a story about a person we will call Carolyn:

Carolyn wanted to be Sunday School superintendent at church. She was involved in teaching Sunday School for years, she helped with all the Christmas Pageants, participated in vacation Bible school and even gave input into the curriculum. When the current superintendent relinquished the position, the president of the church board of directors appointed someone else who wasn't nearly as experienced as Carolyn was. Carolyn suspected that the president of the congregation did not like her much and she felt betrayed. No one else did as much for the Sunday School as she did and not only should she have been appointed, but others should have stood up for her. The woman they appointed didn't even have any children.

Carolyn did not know exactly why she did not get the position, she just got angry and somewhat vindictive. In order to get over all the hurt feelings, she needed to learn and understand why this happened. She could have gone to the president of the congregation or another member of the board and even the minister. It turned out Carolyn was actually considered for the position, but because she had two jobs, was raising two teenagers and a grandchild and her husband was sick, the board thought she had her hands full. There was no animosity, just concern for her. It was easy for her to forgive once she knew what was really going on and now she and the president of the congregation are fast friends. Understanding and learning about the entire story was necessary for forgiveness.

Oprah Winfrey Life Classes are usually very interesting and when Bishop T. D. Jakes was asked how to forgive someone that continually keeps hurting you; he came up with an interesting analogy about quart and pint people that might help you to learn why it keeps happening. Check out this YouTube video, <u>Bishop T.D. Jakes on How to Forgive a Repeat Offender</u>, by OWN TV.

When you are betrayed, you may feel you are being tested. Buddhists believe that those who have the most adversity in life are much closer to enlightenment than others. Try to learn what you are being tested for. Is it because you are impatient and need to learn how to have patience? Take a look at strengths you may develop because of the situation.

Here is a story about a person we will call Dwayne:

Dwayne was pretty useless around the house. He was really bad at cooking, had no idea how to do laundry and never even paid his bills on time. His wife did all that and took care of the kids. She apparently had enough and left him and the kids for a younger man. It was a terrible betrayal, but because of it, he learned many things. He learned how to cook and clean. He learned to pay the bills, he learned how to have a much better relationship with his kids. Forgiving his ex-wife was difficult, but after a while it wasn't so hard. He actually had to thank her and the guy that lured her away for all the things he gained. This betrayal resulted in a learning experience that actually enhanced his life.

We learn from the past, so take past experiences and learn from them. Many times we can apply what we know to a new situation. It puts a new light on things and helps us to resolve our issues quickly and allows us to forgive much quicker.

Learn From Experience

Remember Joe who took credit for our ideas at work? He did what he did purely to get ahead and didn't care about anyone else. However, you got a better job so you forgave him for helping you out, even if that wasn't intentional. Now you see the same thing happening again with another coworker. All of a sudden he is taking credit for your ideas. Learn from that first experience and don't let it happen again. Make sure you get credit for the work you do. You already learned from that experience.

Ask for Advice

Learn from someone who has been in a similar situation. You could talk to a coworker that was also affected by Joe to see how they let go of the anger and pain of betrayal. They may be able to shed new light on the situation and you will learn to be able to forgive. You can also hire a life coach, a counselor, talk to a friend, read a book, or research online.

Define Forgiveness

Do a little research about forgiveness and write down some quotes and a definition on index cards. Stick these cards on your refrigerator where you can see them every day. Understanding and learning forgiveness helps us to forgive.

Counseling

Seek counseling if you just can't forgive someone and want to. A therapist is trained to help you to understand the problem and the need for resolution for yourself and the offender.

Personal Growth Expert, Noah Hammond, produced a YouTube video called How To Forgive Someone Quickly And Easily. It teaches you principles like understanding that everyone does the best they can with the tools they have and why people do things that hurt others, along with why forgiveness has to start from within so that you can grow to forgive.

Learning to forgive is a hard lesson. It takes time, but the best thing about it is that it gets easier with knowledge, understanding and practice.

Chapter 7 – Forgiving Yourself

The person that is the hardest to forgive is yourself. Some say it is the most difficult part of any 12-step recovery program. People are more apt to forgive another person than to accept what they did to cause pain and anguish. We beat ourselves up more relentlessly than any other person would.

A person we will call Michael loved the rock group The Rolling Stones. He had not been to a concert in years, but when a coworker mentioned they were coming to town to perform, he wanted to go. The coworker explained that tickets were all sold out and if you didn't have them now, you weren't going to be able to get them. He was very disappointed and so was Michael, but Michael's wife had connections to the arena where the performance was to take place. He told his coworker he might be able to get four tickets through his wife. However, when his wife announced she was able to get those four tickets his adult son was there and he and his girlfriend wanted to go. Instead of giving the tickets to the coworker, he lied saying he could not get them. His family went to the concert but Michael had guilty feelings the entire time. He knew he was in trouble when the receptionist at the office saw him there. The whole office, including the coworker that told him about the concert, would know he was there. He got to work early the next day and apologized to the coworker before anyone else could tell him he was at the concert.

Guilt has a way of making life difficult. You replay what you did over and over the same way you replay the situation when you have been betrayed. This might make you sick and depressed and when it does, you must do something about it.

Michael knew if the tables were turned and he was lied to, he probably would have been angry for a while. Michael had a real hard time forgiving himself. He believed that forgiveness of his actions was just a way of letting him get away with the deed, and that was not true. When you forgive yourself, you make a pact to never repeat the situation again.

Michael was able to forgive himself because his coworker forgave him. He told him he wasn't sure he wouldn't have done the same thing himself if his kid asked to go, however, he should not have lied to him about it.

Sometimes forgiving yourself has nothing to do with something you have done that could be avoided. A person brought up to believe that being gay is a bad thing might have a problem forgiving themselves because they realize they are gay. In some cases, this problem leads to severe issues and not being able to forgive themselves leads to illness and sometimes death. A person in this situation really needs to seek counseling in order to be able to forgive themselves and be who they need to be.

An accident can cause a person to have issues forgiving themselves even if it was totally unavoidable. A news story I heard about growing up was about a teenager who was backing out of his driveway one afternoon and the neighbor's three year old darted in back of the car at the same time. He hit the child and this caused damage to the child's spinal cord making it so the child would never walk again. He felt like it was his fault, but there was little he could do to stop the accident. The child was small and he did not see him and it all happened so fast there was no way he could have stopped. This teenage boy could not forgive himself for this act and eventually took his own life.

Those of the Jewish faith have a holiday called Yom Kippur, or the day of atonement. On this day, Jews all over the world fast and reflect on any sins they may have committed over the previous year. The Catholics have confession where they go a priest, confess their sins and receive absolution from God. In many ways, being part of these religions helps one to be able to forgive one's self easier. Those that have not grown up in a culture of self-forgiveness may need a little more help.

Self-Forgiveness List

When you get into a situation where you feel that you cannot forgive yourself, make a list to help you see you that you can forgive yourself.

1. Make a list of all your good qualities and take a good look at them. You may see that you are worth forgiving.

2. List what you learned from the situation that is causing pain. My friend Michael might have listed that what he needed to do was give the tickets to his coworker and he defiantly should not have lied.

3. List what you need to do to make amends. Michael would list that he had to admit to his coworker of his actions and promise he would not lie to him again. He might even want to invite the coworker and his wife to another concert of his choice.

Self-Forgiveness Visualization

Try this exercise and see if it does not help you soften your opinion of yourself.

1. Stop, close your eyes and instead of letting thoughts go wild in your head, concentrate on your breathing. Inhale deeply through the nose and exhale through the mouth. Concentrate only on the breath.

2. Go over the situation in your mind. Review images within a frame as if you are watching it happen on TV.

3. Soften the edges around your image and instead of seeing it in sharp contrast, mellow and mute the image. While everything is softened, accept what happened and let it go.

4. If you are still having trouble, imagine that you are a loved one and your personage is explaining the situation to them. Would your mother or father forgive you for your actions if they knew about them. They most likely would so why won't you?

Steps to Forgiving Yourself

Follow these steps in order to achieve self-forgiveness.

1. Accept your flaws. No one is perfect and your flaws are what make you unique.

2. Remember that you are not a bad person. There is a real difference between doing something bad in order to hurt someone and making a mistake. What makes a person bad is doing a bad thing with intent and hopefully you did not do that.

3. Talk to someone. Get another person's perspective on the situation because your vision might be clouded. Getting support and feedback from someone will help you feel that you deserve to forgive yourself.

4. Talk to your internal voice. Call this voice your consciousness or imaginary friend. Give it a name and explain the situation. It is quite normal for it to talk back to you. Is it giving you suggestions to improve yourself? It might even be trying to protect you.

5. Do the best friend test. Imagine that your best friend did to you what you did to another person. If you would forgive him or her for doing it, you can certainly forgive yourself.

Meditating often helps with self-forgiveness and Jack Kornfield leads a very easy to understand meditation in the below YouTube video. It takes you from relaxation and visualization to reflection and relating to self-forgiveness and asking yourself for forgiveness. It is a 10 minute Forgiveness Meditation posted by Greater Good Science Center that is very easy to do.

Give yourself a break. Some mistakes are just that – mistakes and you need to forgive yourself for them. Maybe you should have known better, but you must accept them, move on and never let them happen again.

Most importantly, decide once and for all that you are not going to waste your life on negative thoughts, emotions, and pain of the past and that instead you are going to work hard every day to forgive and move on! Many of the most successful people in the world have the ability to forgive and keep moving forward with purpose, determination, and a clean heart. Don't let hatred, anger, jealousy, resentment, and other negative emotions rule your life any longer! Take a stand today and fight back from now and here on after!

Conclusion

I hope this book was able to help you to forgive others and forgive yourself.

The next step is to learn that forgiveness has great value and to apply all the techniques and exercises in this book in order to forgive, heal, and move on to a happy life. It is a gift to yourself and to others. It isn't really about blame or fault. It is simply about letting go, completely and permanently, of anger and pain within yourself.

Forgiveness is seeing that what happened just happened and there is no good in allowing it to fester and take over your life and thoughts. Forgiveness erases the slate and gives you and the offender an opportunity to move forward.

Forgiveness does not condone the act, it is not giving in, it is not pretending that nothing happened or it wasn't a big deal. Forgiveness is not justification or a forced action in order to just get along.

Forgiveness is moving forward and choosing peace and happiness. It is the refusal to play the past over and over and the realization that resentment and revenge has no place in your life.

Forgiveness comes with many benefits. Most people will see a decrease in depression and anxiety and forgiveness can increase hope, give self-esteem and a nice sense of well-being. In some cases it creates better relationships and sense of control. In a study conducted in California, subjects were made angry and, during this test, they produced much less immunoglobulin, which is a substance that inhibits the flu and cold virus. The immune system was compromised and they got sick more often. Staying calm tends to help the immune system produce what it needs to keep you healthy. Other studies have shown that people who forgive have better heart function and less stress.

One of the best things about forgiveness is that it is never too early or late to do. You can forgive someone at any time whether it is two weeks or two years from the time it happened. The person you hurt most by fending off forgiveness and stewing in your own misery is yourself.

This YouTube video by Actualized.org, <u>How To Forgive Someone</u>, helps you understand how to make forgiveness stick, so that you don't let the situation come back over and over again.

It is critical that you find the forgiveness exercises that work best for you, and do them every day for at least two weeks, and if it is a serious issue, than a month or however long it takes. Forgiveness does not come easily to many people, so by making forgiveness a habit that you do every day, you will be amazed at the incredible results that you have over time! I would also recommend checking out the variety of free "Tapping" videos on YouTube as they can be quite helpful.

Being consistent is the key! If you would like more advanced knowledge on how to make key behavior's a habit, check out my bestselling book: The Top 100 Best Habits.

Desmond Tutu said, "Forgiveness says you are given another chance to make a new beginning." Whether you are forgiving someone else or yourself, make a new start today to a better and more productive life.

Finally, if you discovered at least one thing that has helped you or that you think would be beneficial to someone else, be sure to take a few seconds to easily post a quick positive review. As an author, your positive feedback is desperately needed. Your highly valuable five star reviews are like a river of golden joy flowing through a sunny forest of mighty trees and beautiful flowers! *To do your good deed in making the world a better place by helping others with your valuable insight, just leave a nice review.*

My Other Books and Audio Books
www.AcesEbooks.com

Peak Performance Books

SUCCESS
SUCCESS STRATEGIES

THE TOP 100 BEST WAYS TO BE SUCCESSFUL

Ace McCloud

Ace McCloud

HABIT

The Top 100 Best Habits
How To Make A Positive Habit Permanent
And How To Break Bad Habits

MOTIVATION

MASTER THE POWER OF MOTIVATION
TO PROPEL YOURSELF TO SUCCESS

Ace McCloud

ATTITUDE

Discover The True Power Of
A Positive Attitude

Ace McCloud

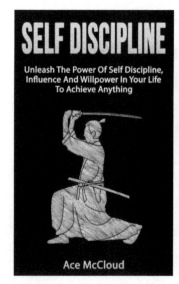

SELF DISCIPLINE

Unleash The Power Of Self Discipline,
Influence And Willpower In Your Life
To Achieve Anything

Ace McCloud

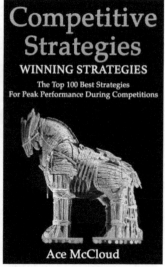

Competitive Strategies
WINNING STRATEGIES

The Top 100 Best Strategies
For Peak Performance During Competitions

Ace McCloud

Health Books

ULTIMATE HEALTH SECRETS

HEALTH

Strategies For Dieting, Eating Healthy, Exercising, Losing Weight, The Mediterranean Diet, Strength Training, And All About Vitamins, Minerals, And Supplements

Ace McCloud

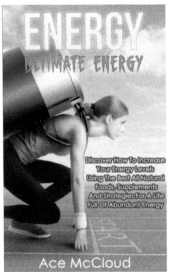

ENERGY
ULTIMATE ENERGY

Discover How To Increase Your Energy Levels Using The Best All Natural Foods, Supplements And Strategies For A Life Full Of Abundant Energy

Ace McCloud

RECIPE BOOK

The Best Food Recipes That Are Delicious, Healthy, Great For Energy And Easy To Make

Ace McCloud

MASSAGE THERAPY

TRIGGER POINT THERAPY
ACUPRESSURE THERAPY
Learn The Best Techniques For Optimum Pain Relief And Relaxation

Ace McCloud

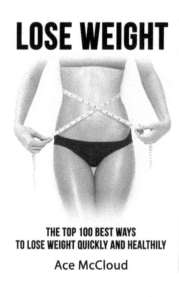

Be sure to check out my audio books as well!

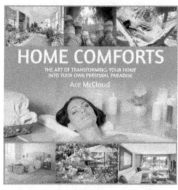

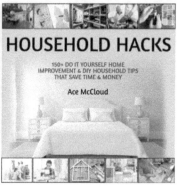

Check out my website at: **www.AcesEbooks.com** for a complete list of all of my books and high quality audio books. I enjoy bringing you the best knowledge in the world and wish you the best in using this information to make your journey through life better and more enjoyable! **Best of luck to you!**

Lightning Source UK Ltd.
Milton Keynes UK
UKHW031301110521
383484UK00007B/1117